SHARK LIFE

written by Annabel Griffin

illustrated by Rose Wilkinson

First published in 2022 by Hungry Tomato Ltd
F15, Old Bakery Studios, Blewetts Wharf, Malpas Road, Truro, Cornwall, TR1 1QH, UK.

A CIP catalog record for this book is available from the British Library.

ISBN 978-1-915461-08-7

Manufactured in the USA.

Discover more at
www.hungrytomato.com

CONTENTS

Words in **bold** can be found in the glossary.

SHARK LIFE

Sharks are awesome! Did you know there are over 500 different types? Each one has incredible features that help them survive life in the ocean.

Special skills

Sharks have been ruling the seas for millions of years. In that time, many have **evolved** to have some amazing skills. Did you know some sharks can even glow in the dark?

Smart hunters

Almost all sharks are **carnivores**, and many are incredible hunters with super sharp senses, and teeth!

Where to find them

Sharks can be found in every ocean on Earth. Some live up near the surface, while others hide out in the darkest deep-sea waters.

SEA MONSTERS OF THE PAST

Hundreds of millions of years before dinosaurs roamed the Earth, some sharks were already swimming in the oceans!

Buzz-saw jaw

Helicoprion had a spiral of teeth in its lower jaw, which it used to slice through its **prey**.

Ancient ancestor

Even though they lived 360 million years ago, *Cladoselache* had quite a lot in common with modern sharks.

Ironing board shark

Stethacanthus had a large, strangely shaped fin on its back.

Shark Timeline:

(mya = millions of years ago)

450 mya
Evidence exists of shark **ancestors** this far back

410 mya
Acanthodians evolve (ancient shark ancestors)

380 mya
Cladoselache evolves

Mega shark!

The biggest ever shark, the *Megalodon* was probably between 50 – 60 feet (15 – 18 m) long. Thats over three times longer than the largest *great white shark*!

360 mya
Stethacanthus and *Helicoprion* evolve

243 mya
The first dinosaurs start to appear

200-145 mya
The *Jurassic Period*. Most modern shark groups develop in this period.

20 mya
Megalodon and first *hammerhead sharks* evolve

SHARK BODIES

Sharks are perfectly designed for swimming through water. While they come in different shapes and sizes, they all have similar features.

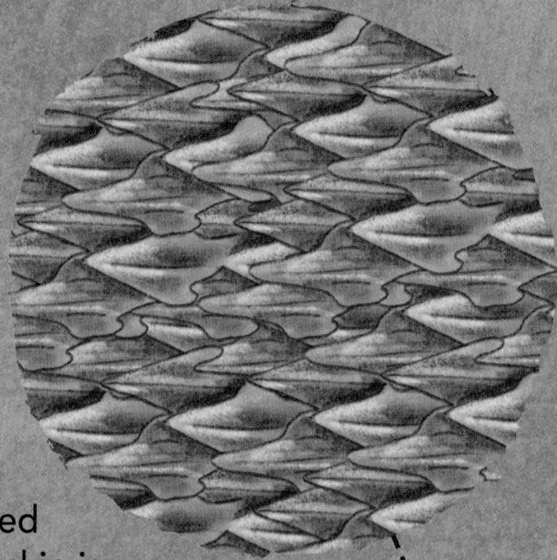

Skin

Shark skin is covered in tiny scales called *denticles*. The skin is rough to touch, but helps the shark swim faster.

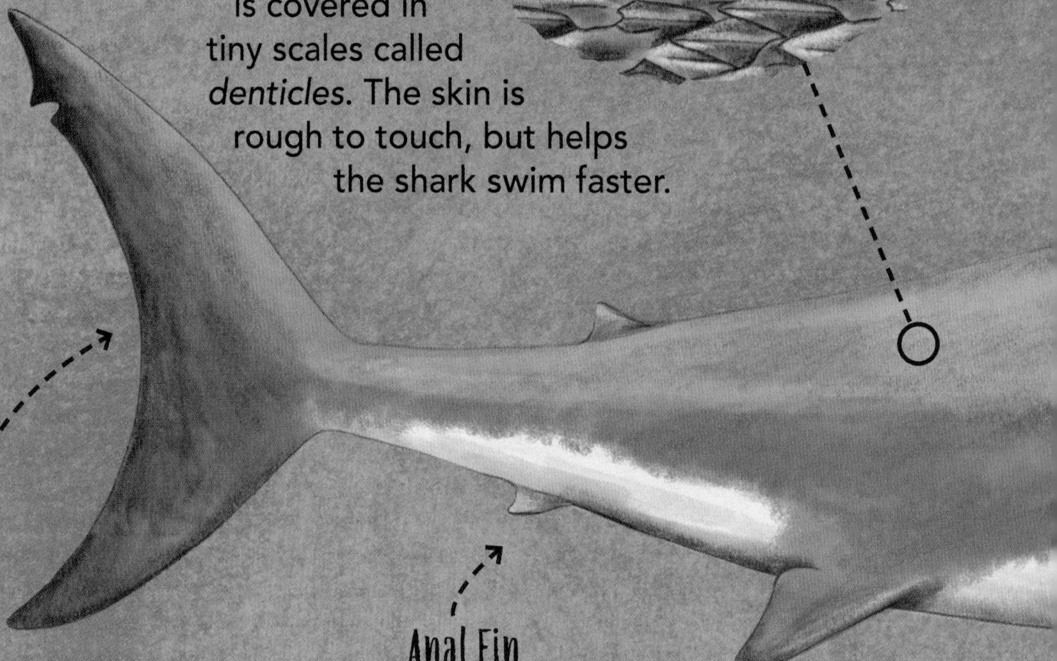

Anal Fin

Pelvic Fin

Tail

A shark's tail is for speed and forward movement. *Thresher sharks* also use their extra-long tails as a weapon.

Dorsal Fin

Helps keep the shark steady.

Skeleton

Shark skeletons aren't made of bone. They are made of **cartilage**, which is much lighter and more flexible. Our noses and ears are made from the same stuff!

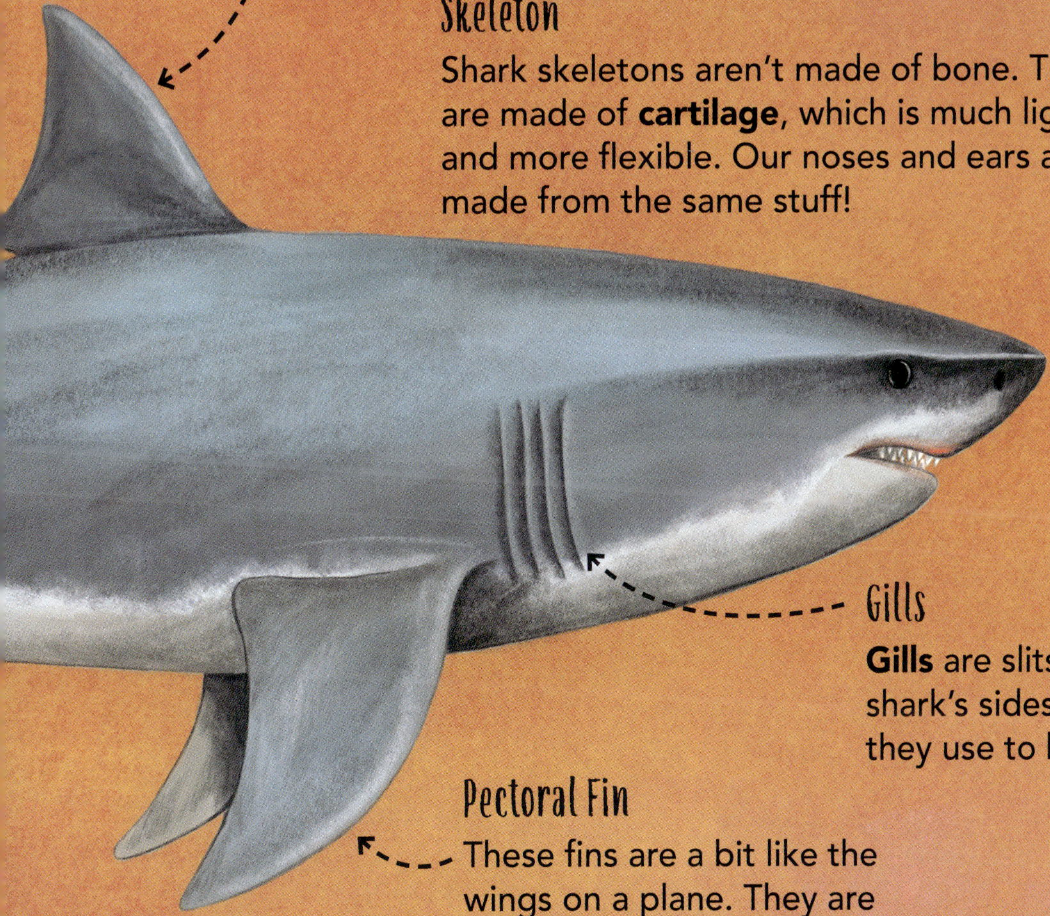

Gills

Gills are slits in a shark's sides, which they use to breathe.

Pectoral Fin

These fins are a bit like the wings on a plane. They are used for balance and steering.

SUPER SENSES

Sharks are quick and clever hunters. They use their super strong senses to find and catch their prey.

Hearing

Shark ears are tiny little holes in the side of their head. But don't let that fool you, they've got great hearing.

Electro-location

A shark's **snout** is covered in tiny jelly-filled pores, called *ampullae of Lorenzini*. They can sense tiny electrical currents in the water.

Smell

A shark could smell just one drop of blood mixed with one million drops of water!

Sight

Having eyes far apart on the side of their heads means that sharks can see in almost all directions.

Tiger shark

Lunch bell?

Some sharks have barbels hanging down from their snouts. These help them find prey.

Blind shark

barbel

TEETH AND JAWS

A shark's teeth are its greatest weapon, so it's important for them to have a nice sharp set at all times.

Out with the old...

Some sharks lose 30,000 teeth in their lifetime! They replace them regularly as they are easily damaged.

...In with the new

They have many rows of teeth and make new ones all the time. When a tooth falls out, the one behind moves forward to take its place.

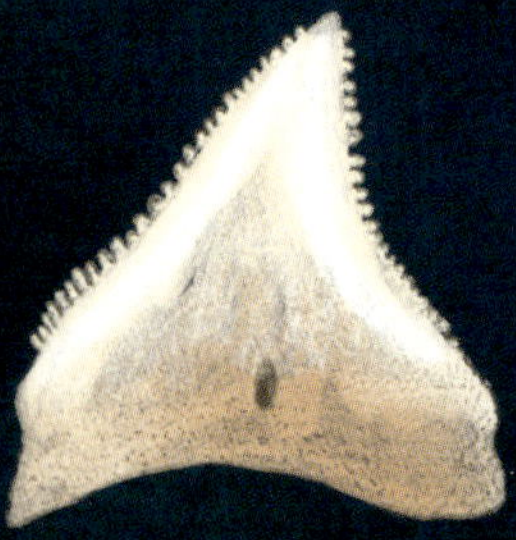

Tiger shark tooth

Sevengill cow shark tooth

Bull shark tooth

Jutting Jaws

Some sharks, like the *great white*, have a jaw that isn't firmly attached to their skull. This means they can push it forward to take big, powerful bites.

Great white shark jaw

Some shark teeth have **serrated** edges to tear through flesh.

Great white shark tooth

Long, thin teeth are good for piercing and holding onto prey.

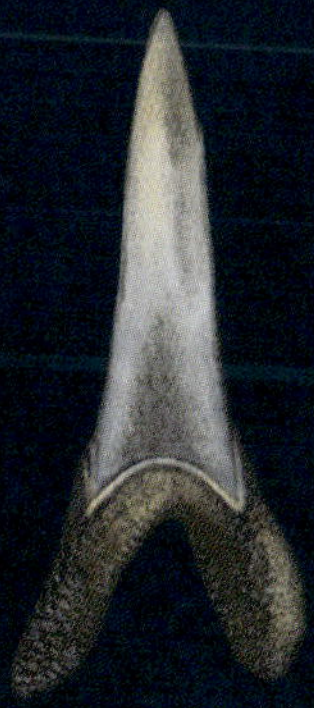

Sand tiger shark tooth

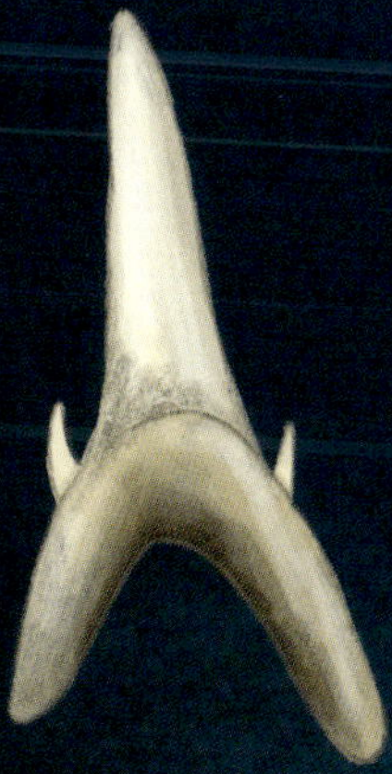

Goblin shark tooth

Whale sharks have around 3,000 tiny teeth, but they don't actually use them!

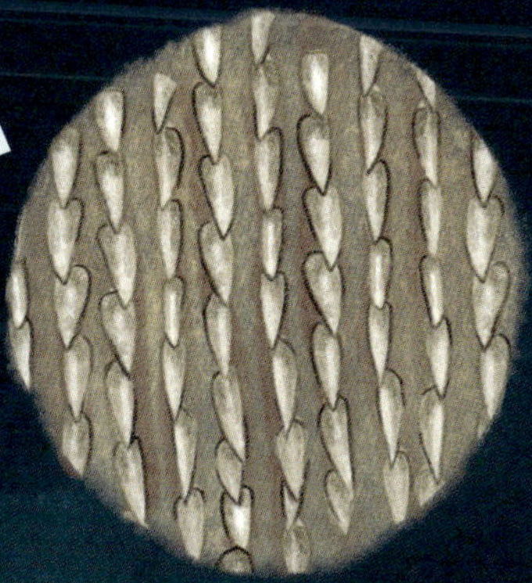

A section of whale shark teeth

BABY SHARKS

Baby sharks are called pups. Some sharks give birth to live pups, while others lay eggs.

Shark nurseries

Some sharks lay eggs, or give birth, in safe waters, known as *nurseries*. Nurseries offer pups protection until they are old enough to defend themselves.

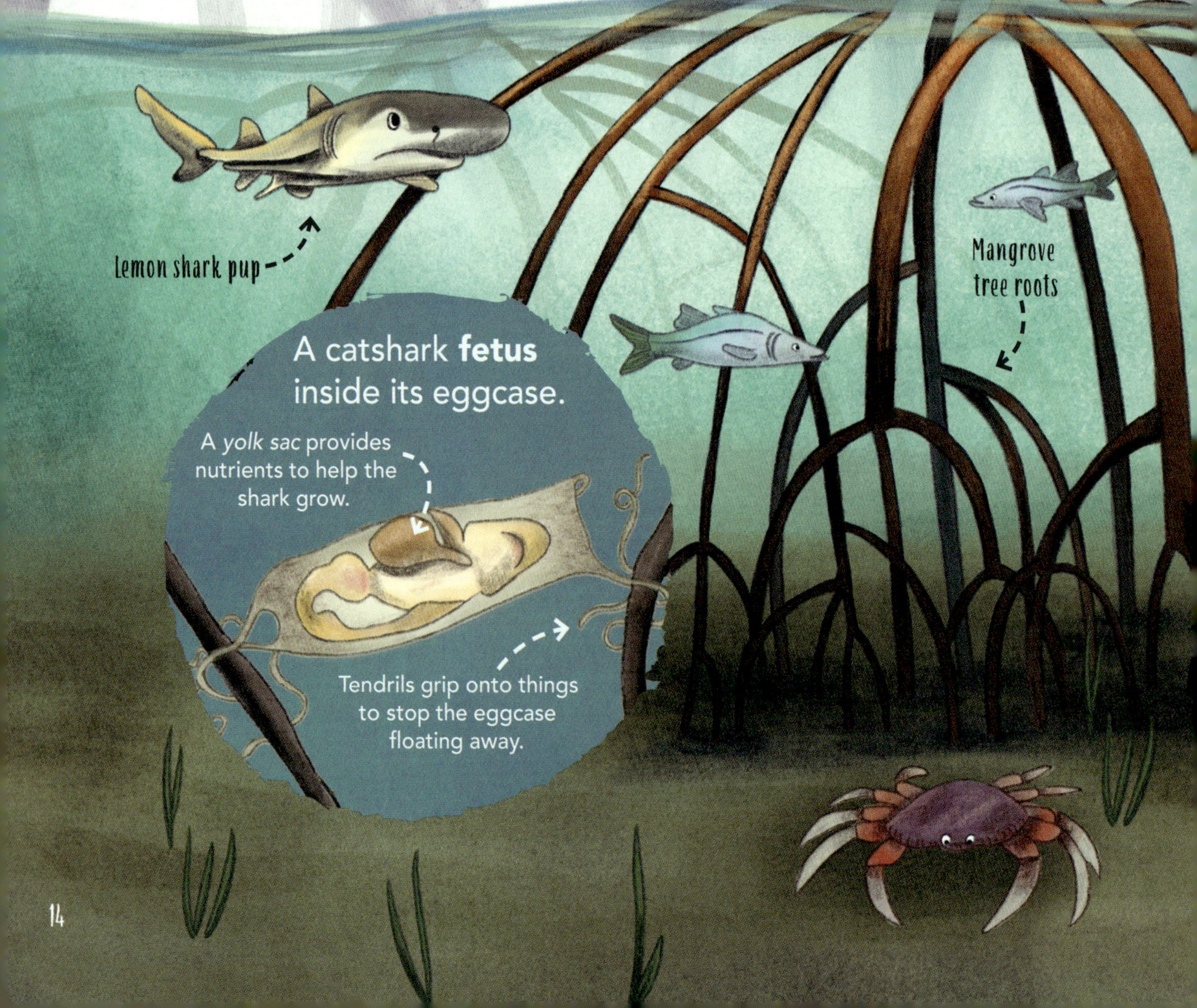

Underwater treehouse

Mangrove forests, like this one, make good nurseries. The tree roots are the perfect pup hideout. No big **predators** allowed!

Mermaids' Purses

An empty eggcase is known as a *mermaid's purse*. You can tell what kind of shark hatched, based on the shape.

Large spotted catshark

Ghost shark (chimaera)

Australian swellshark

Horn shark

WHO DIVES DEEPEST?

Some sharks have been known to dive to incredible depths in the ocean.

3,280 ft
(1,000 m)

Midnight zone

Oceanic whitetip shark
Dive range: 0 – 3,550 ft (0 – 1,080 m)

Great white shark
Dive range: 0 – 3,940 ft (0 – 1,200 m)

Basking shark
Dive range: 0 – 4,140 ft (0 – 1,260 m)

Goblin shark
Dive range: 0 – 4,260 ft (0 – 1,300 m)

Frilled shark
Dive range: 160 – 4,920 ft (50 – 1,500 m)

Whale shark
Dive range: 0 – 6,320 ft (0 – 1,930 m)

Cookiecutter shark
Dive range: 0 – 11,480 ft (0 – 3,500 m)

Greenland shark
Dive range: 0 – 8,680 ft (0 – 2,650 m)

The deeper you dive, the darker it gets. The ocean is split into zones according to the amount of sunlight there is. There is complete darkness in the midnight zone.

WHAT'S THAT SHARK?

Scientists split sharks into different groups, according to their physical **characteristics.** This flow chart will help you identify some of the most commonly seen types of shark.

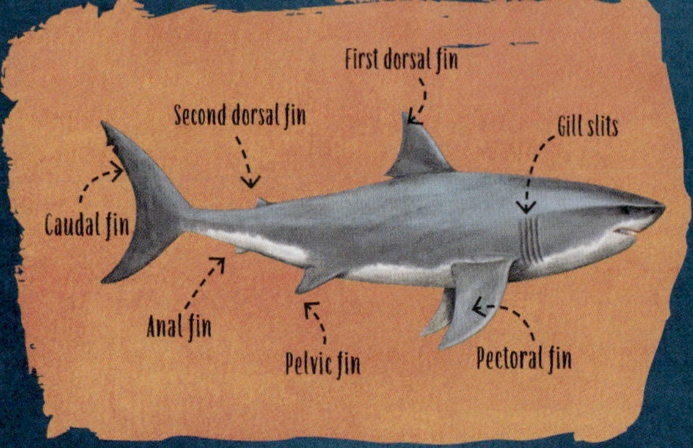

START

Does the shark have an anal fin? → NO

NO ↓ Is its body flat? → YES → It's one of 22 different types of *angel shark.* →

Angel shark (Squatina squatina)

Is its body flat? ↓ NO → It's a *dogfish shark.* →

Spiny dogfish shark

Does the shark have an anal fin? ↓ YES

Does it have one dorsal fin and six or seven pairs of gill slits? → YES → It's a *cow shark.* →

Broadnose seven gill cow shark

↓ NO →

It's a *mackerel shark*, a group that includes the great white and mako sharks.

Great white shark

NO

Does it have a nictating eyelid (an extra eyelid that closes for protection)? → YES → It's one of nearly 300 different types of *ground shark*.

Tiger shark

NO

Is its mouth in front of its eyes? → YES → It's a *carpet shark*. Members of this group come in lots of different sizes.

Whale shark

NO

Does it have dorsal fins with spines on them? → YES → It's a *bullhead shark*. There are only nine different types.

Horn shark

SHARK LIFE FACTS

Slow starters

Most sharks grow up slowly, and it takes a long time before they are ready to have their own pups. Greenland sharks only have young when they are over 100 years old!

Greenland Shark

Sand tiger shark pups eat their siblings in the womb.

Born to hunt

Some sharks start hunting before they are even born! They will attack their siblings from inside the **womb.**

Blue sharks

Life in black and white

Sharks may have good eyesight, but they are thought to be completely color blind.

Where has the megalodon gone?

The invincible-looking giant probably became **extinct** 3.6 million years ago. No one knows for sure what happened, but some scientists think the rise of great white sharks was to blame.

Megalodon

GLOSSARY

ancestors
Members of a family from long ago. For instance, your great great grandmother would be an ancestor of yours.

carnivores
Animals that mostly eat meat.

cartilage
A flexible material that makes up part of many animals' bodies, including humans. Shark skeletons are made of it.

characteristics
Physical features or behaviors that make something, or someone, recognizable.

evolved
Having changed or developed slowly over a long period of time.

extinct
When a type of plant or animal no longer exists anywhere on Earth.

fetus
An unborn or unhatched baby animal.

gills
A body part that sharks, and other fish, use to breathe underwater.

predators
An animal that hunts and kills other animals for food.

prey
An animal that is hunted and killed by other animals for food.

serrated
Sharp, zig-zagged points along the edge of something, like a saw.

snout
A long nose that sticks out from the rest of the head.

womb
A part inside some animals where babies grow before they are born.

INDEX

About the Author

Annabel is a writer and artist based in Cornwall, UK, who writes children's books with a focus on animals and the natural world. She is the author of the *One Planet* series, about Earth and the environment, and *What Can I See in the Wild?*, published by Beetle Books. In her free time, Annabel enjoys drawing, hiking, and gardening. She is never without a good book.

About the Illustrator

Rose is an illustrator, artist and educator from Hereford, UK, now living and working in London. Her mediums of choice are watercolor, gouache, pencil and Procreate.

Picture Credits

(abbreviations: t = top; b = bottom; c = center; l = left; r = right)

Shutterstock: Aleksei Lazukov 18tr; Boris Pamikov 18cr; Wildestanimal 18br; Davidpstephens 19tr; Michael Bogner 19tr; Manamana 19br; Enessa Varnaeva 19br; Dotted Yeti 20tr; Valeri Potapova 20cl; Martin Prochazkacz 21tl; warpaint 21bc.

Every effort has been made to trace the copyright holders, and we apologize in advance for any unintentional omissions. We would be pleased to insert the appropriate acknowledgments in any subsequent edition of this publication.